M

MW01196543

# *Discovering*
# Corn Dollies

*Drawings by R. C. Lambeth*

# SHIRE PUBLICATIONS LTD.

# Contents

The late author acknowledged the help she received from the following: the Museum of Man, USA; Mrs Charlotte Johnson, USA; and Mrs E. Lamoureux, Canada, for the group of Mexican Angels; the late Edwin Smith for his wonderful photographs; the Japanese Information Centre and the Hong Kong Government for photographs and information about the Japanese straw smocks; Dorothy Wright for basketry information; the Museum of English Rural Life, Reading University, for permission to include photographs of items in their collection; and her late husband, R. C. Lambeth, for drawing the illustrations of corn dollies.
Photographs are acknowledged as follows: the late Edwin Smith, plates 1, 2, and 7; Bruce, plate 6; Charlotte Johnson, plates 3 and 5; Dorothy Wright, plate 8; the late M. Lambeth, plate 4; the late R. C. Lambeth, plate 9.

Cover design by Ron Shaddock, based on illustrations by R. C. Lambeth.

*Published in 1994 by Shire Publications Ltd, Cromwell House, Church Street, Princes Risborough, Buckinghamshire HP27 9AJ, UK.*
*Copyright © 1994 by Shire Publications Ltd. First published 1974; reprinted 1974, 1975, 1977, 1979, 1982, 1985, 1987, 1990 and 1994. Number 199 in the 'Discovering' series. ISBN 0 85263 283 5.*

Printed in Great Britain by CIT Printing Services, Press Buildings, Merlins Bridge, Haverfordwest, Dyfed SA61 1XF.

# 1. Legends and traditions

Almost everyone has heard of corn dollies but what brought them into being and why were they considered so important? Many myths and legends from many lands tell the stories of how ancient people learned the art of grain cultivation, of their efforts to explain what caused the plants to grow and produce yet more seeds, and of their attempts to please the gods with gifts at each season in expectation of good harvests.

Long before people recorded the history of their countries on tablets or in books they recounted the things which had occurred, to their children and grandchildren, each generation adding a little more knowledge to the stories. The sun, moon and the elements became gods to be appeased with gifts and sacrifices, and these must be taken into account when considering the emblems offered in thankfulness at harvest ingathering.

First came the Creator, sometimes a father, sometimes a mother, who created everything man needed, and taught him how to make use of them.

It is thought by many people that grain was first cultivated in Egypt, but the myths of other countries tell similar stories; it is known barley and rye grew wild in many of them.

The Egyptian legend tells how an early king taught his people to cultivate both wheat and barley. He was Osiris and his wife was Isis; both were later worshipped as gods by their people. The story tells that Isis drew her husband's attention to the wheat and barley growing wild. Osiris then taught his people to break up the land in the Nile valley after the annual flood had receded to sow the seed and later to reap the harvest.

Another Egyptian god, Tefnut, was called 'the spitter' because he was the rain, while a fish deity Rem, whose name means 'to weep', was thought to weep fertilising tears. The connection between a fish god and a corn god is understandable for in Egypt and Babylon the harvest was considered a gift from the river.

In Babylon the myth of how corn was brought under cultivation brings the same story. Ea-Oannes, a wise man-cum-god instructed his people in all things, including the cultivation of grain. Ishtar, the mother of the Universe, was thought to supply the food of animals and mankind and it was her son Tammuz who became the corn spirit. The people described him as the young god who died each year yet returned to life, as the spirit in the seed which awoke to life and growth after the spring sowing. He was thought to slay the demons of winter and bad weather, making it possible for man to proceed with ploughing and sowing. Likewise in India, Indra fought Vritra and the drought demons,

3

and in Scandinavia Thor fought and overcame the frost giants. Each of these corn spirits received offerings of human sacrifices at first; later animals were substituted and, with the growth of civilisation, the offerings became food and drink made from the newly harvested grain. In the book of Exodus, xxiii,16 and 19, we are told 'And the feast of harvest, the first fruits of thy labours, which thou hast sown in the field: and the feast of ingathering, which is in the end of the year, ... the first fruits of thy land thou shalt bring into the house of the Lord thy God'. All people offered their 'first fruits' from their harvest to their god, and it was usual to decorate the offering.

Because early people realised the necessity of moisture to germinate the seeds they thought it part of the ritual of sowing that the sower should weep and so all corn deities were weeping gods, who shed fertilising tears. David in the Psalms writes 'They that sow in tears shall reap in joy. He that goeth forth and weepeth, bearing precious seed, shall doubtless come again with rejoicing bringing his sheaves with him.'

In India the legend is that Indra, as the thunder god, brought rain to the dried up pastures of the Punjab. He was the corn spirit and the god of fertility. After his battle with the drought demons the clouds poured forth the rain which revived the earth and so fed the maturing rice harvest. At their barley harvest in the spring and again with the reaping of the rice in the autumn the people offered their thanks to the gods. A special cake of bread made with the new grain was offered to Indra and to the god Agni who had brought the sown seed to life. Dyaus-Pita, god of heaven, and Prithivee, mother earth, were offered a cake containing butter or sometimes just butter, for butter was considered to be the sap of heaven and earth. All the lesser gods were offered a mixture made of old grain boiled in milk and water.

In India today straw designs are made mainly with rice straw and used as talismans or charms, often found hanging in the doorways of homes in which newly married couples are about to take up residence. The designs are based on objects in common use such as purses or combs. They also make the ram's horn which is a mythical emblem signifying a plentiful supply of food.

In Greece, this cornucopia, or ram's horn, was supposed to be the creation of Zeus. He wanted a thank offering for nymphs who cared for him as a baby so he took a ram's horn and filled it with the best of nature's edible seeds and gave it with the promise that the contents would supply all the food they required. Zeus, like the corn spirits of other lands, was said to die a violent death each year and be reborn. This is the cycle of ploughing, sowing, and reaping.

China and Japan also have these same stories of early cultivation and irrigation. In the Kurashiki Museum in Japan are smocks made of straw such as would be worn by people working in the rice fields. The Japanese made fine straw figures of warriors.

The Teutonic legend differs in its story and implies a later period, for we are told Frey, the god of harvest, gave a sheaf of golden corn to Heimdal, the keeper of the bridge Bif-rost (the rainbow), when he came into the world as a child. Heimdal made himself small and lay down in a boat with his head pillowed on the sheaf of wheat for his journey. One day a boat was seen approaching the shores of Scedeland. In it lay a small child asleep with his head on a sheaf of grain. The people took the child and brought him up, giving him the name Scyld (Scef) meaning 'of the sheaf'. Scyld taught them how to grow the seed from the sheaf. At the end of his life as a human he requested the people to put his body in a boat such as the one he came in and set it afloat on the sea. This they did, putting many thank offerings for the harvest around him and leaving the boat to drift away.

The interest of the Teutonic myth lies in the suggestion of wheat being brought by sea from some other country. That the sheaf was treated with honour would account for corn dollies being made in this shape.

The myths given here tell how people tried to explain the wonders of Nature, how our food evolved and why they made corn dollies. These harvest emblems were thank offerings to their gods or idols and it is from the word idol that the name dolly comes. First the shapes made were sheaves or bunches of corn decorated with wild flowers and sprays of green leaves, then, as can be seen from some of the early names given to them in different countries, these evolved into roughly made figures. Mother Earth is probably the best known today but old names include Harvest Dame, Maiden, Old Man, Hag, Cripple Goat, Harvest Queen. In France at the time of Henry IV the peasants called their straw figure and their supper the Harvest Gosling, while in Poland the last handful of grain cut was bound up and called a Quail.

All countries had a custom of 'cutting the last handful of corn' in the field. In Britain it varied from county to county; some preferred to throw their sickles at it until there was nothing left, others thought it held an evil spirit and trampled it into the ground. Many treated it with honour for they believed the corn spirit had retreated into it as a refuge when the rest of the crop was cut. In this the corn spirit was thought to sleep throughout the winter. In the spring it was taken to the fields when seed was being sown, so that the spirit could transfer to the sown seed and awaken it. This explains why countries spoke of their belief that the corn spirit died each year and was reborn the following spring and why they held ceremonies at ploughing and seed time.

Corn dollies are the outcome of harvest, a way of saying thank you for the crops. This 'thank you' begins much earlier in the year when a service is held to bless the ploughs, usually on the Sunday before 'Plough Monday', the Monday following twelfth night after Christmas. Years ago this was considered the beginning of the countrymen's year and was celebrated by ploughboys and their friends as a holiday, when they took their plough into the streets of nearby towns. They dressed in fancy clothes, some as women, one as a fool, and they blackened their faces, teasing the townspeople into giving contributions of money by threatening to plough up their garden paths or doorsteps. In the evening they made merry at the village inn, drinking away the money they had spent the day collecting.

Today this ceremony has changed a little, for money collected usually goes to charity, but the old wooden plough is brought from its resting place at the back of someone's barn or the church tower for this one day. (A tractor pulling a modern plough would be out of place in so old a custom.) The one used at Balsham in Cambridgeshire is though to be 200 years old. The Morris Men in their ribbon-trimmed clothes and jingling bells added to the procession as they performed their traditional dances. The two figures, Betsy and her Mate, collected 'donations' in their 'vittle bags' to the cries of 'Pity the poor plough-boy', and 'Hurrah' if coins were given, but a howl of 'Hunger and starvation' if they were refused.

According to Bloomfield's *History of Norfolk* the procession is the remains of an old custom in which people placed 'plough lights' before the figures of saints in their churches. To get the money for these lights they 'Took their plough into the streets, dancing and miming for coppers'. The practice of the lights in the church was stopped during Cromwell's protectorate but the processions continued.

Other days highlighted in the farming year were a feast of seedcake, pasties and furmety pot at the end of wheat sowing; Shrove Tuesday when they 'threshed' the fat hen; and after sheep shearing, a supper; the 'cream pot' or churn supper when all the corn was cut but not yet stored; and the harvest supper when all was safely stacked for the winter.

The harvest supper had many names and traditional customs but always the sheaf last cut was part of the merry making, sometimes as a crude female figure, the 'Dame' in Yorkshire where the supper was called 'The Innings Goose' because the main dish of the meal was roast goose. This special sheaf was then given to the winner of a race run by all those who had taken part in the work of harvest.

Another reference to the goose comes from Shropshire where the cutting of the last handful of standing corn was called 'cutting the gander's neck'. In ancient times the goose was identified with the corn spirit and it was thought she laid the 'sun egg'. In Scotland this harvest supper had a custom whereby the sheaf, dressed as a 'maiden', was brought into the room by the prettiest girl who then became 'Queen of the Maiden Feast'. In Norfolk the figure was brought home in procession from the field on the last, or horkey, load and was known as 'Ben' the meaning of which appears to be 'the best'. The food for their supper was roast beef followed by plum pudding with plenty of ale to wash it down. After the meal the men took a large jug of ale into one of the fields for their ceremony of crying 'Hello Largess' where they formed a ring round the man with the jug who blew on a horn as they swung their joined hands up high. After three calls they all drank from the jug.

In some counties this toasting was part of the Christmas rejoicing, as in Devon where the cider trees were honoured or in counties where the new crops received the toast. The lighting of fires in the wheat fields on Twelfth Night Eve would appear to be a relic of honouring the Magi although with the passing of the centuries this reason was forgotten and was replaced by the belief that toasting the new wheat crops protected them from disease.

Scotland had one special day which England does not follow. In the Western Islands on February 2nd each family would dress up a sheaf of oats and put it in a basket by the hearth before going to bed at night. A club was left with it for Brud and after saying 'Brud is welcome' they retired. Next morning they looked to see if Brud had used her club to leave a mark in the ashes as a sign of good crops for the year. Why this sheaf was dressed as a woman or why she was called Brud is unknown.

# 2. Basic plaiting

Before beginning to make corn dollies it is important for the plaiter to learn something about the type of straw required to produce good even work. Old and damaged straw, solid stemmed straw and badly discoloured straw should never be used. Only hollow stemmed straw will satisfy the expert, so learn as much as possible of the different varieties, the old, and the new. Rye is the whitest in colour but it is also harder to work with. Oats are hollow stemmed but softer. Wheat is probably the best and easiest straw for the beginner, provided you make sure you have chosen a hollow stemmed variety. Years ago straw was mostly hollow but with the coming of the combine many varieties, produced in the 1930s and subsequently, had solid stems. New varieties coming on the market today are hollow but the length of plaiting straw is shorter and this means more joins in the work.

First class plaiting is done with the top length of the stem, that is the piece from the ear down to where the last leaf leaves the stem. Cutting this piece off each stem is one of the chores which pay. Strip off any dead leaves and then sort the straws into at least three groups, thick, medium and fine (more if you have the time). This grading will prove useful in at least two ways, first it will help you make a more even plait, secondly it gives you the chance to use the thicker straws for big dollies which need bold plait and to keep very fine straws for small and delicate designs.

The beginner will find the five straw plait the best to work with for this produces a four sided or square plait. Start by tying five straws together close to the ears, as shown in Fig. 1. The fifth straw is to help in moving on from one corner fold to the next. Each time the straw being folded passes over two corners, it is then left and the one at the last corner is picked up and used in its place until the round is complete. In Fig. 1 we have used N, S, E and W to help with this round and the five drawings give the positions of the straws as you work the round. The illustrated loop of plait shows what this looks like when working without a core. Fig. 2 shows the same plait worked round a core and the dolly when finished. One thing it is well to realise from the beginning is that the spiral which forms the attractive pattern is the natural outcome of round succeeding round.

Because most plaiting is done long after the corn has been cut in the field, the straw is dry and somewhat hard. This means damping the straw as you need it. Place as much as you require each time flat in a sink or other container big enough to allow the straws sufficient room. Then cover with cold water for about fifteen minutes. Stand the straws upright so that the surplus water can drain away and they are ready for use.

Once you have learnt to make a good even plait try experimenting with more straws in each round. For the shaping of bells, candlesticks and lanterns, where the size of the rounds has to get progressively larger, the straw being folded must be placed to the outside of the second straw it passes (Fig. 3, a) but for drawing the rounds in smaller the straw which is being folded must come to rest inside the second one as in Fig. 3, b. Care must be taken in both these techniques not to draw in, or widen out, too quickly as this will result in gaps in the plait which spoils the look of the work.

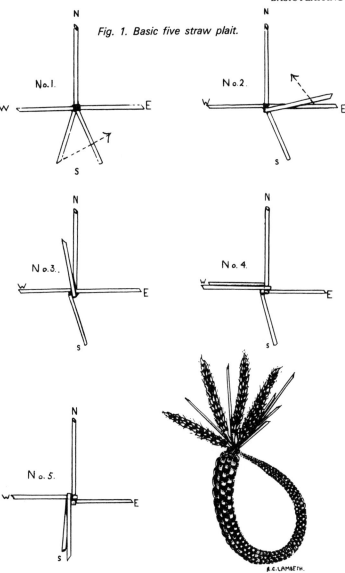

*Fig. 1. Basic five straw plait.*

A.C. LAMBETH.

9

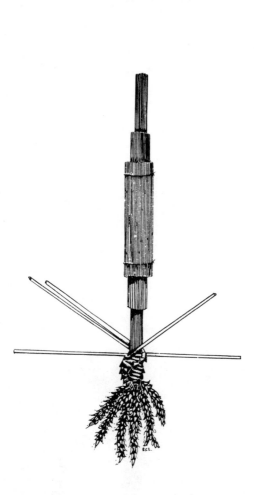

*Fig. 2. Plaiting a traditional dolly core, and completed dolly.*

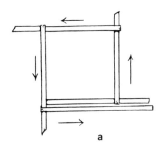

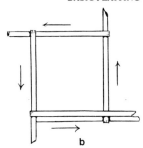

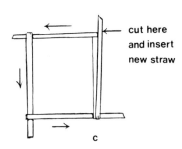

cut here
and insert
new straw

*Fig. 3. Narrowing and widening plaits, and inserting a new straw.*

Spider web plaiting, as the name implies, produces a flat surface but very much closer than a spider spins his web. The ribs this is worked on vary according to the size of 'tablet' required and the work is done with one straw, taking it from rib to rib, wrapping it round each in turn, as shown in the basket in plate 1.

Feeding in new straws is done in the same way for all work, the old straw being cut off after it has passed the second straw. The thin end of a new straw is inserted in the hole, making sure of a firm fit which is hidden under the fold of the straw of the next round (Fig. 3, c).

## The traditional dolly or Neck

This particular design is one of the simplest and yet the most popular corn dolly of them all. It can be given a different look in so many ways while retaining its original shape. It can be made with or without a core but I have found more people choose the solid one than the hollow variety. The core is simple to make. Tie firmly together a good bunch of straws still bearing the corn ears; then add two or three rounds more of straws without ears, each round of straws being shorter than the previous round. This gives a pleasant shape to the finished object. It can then be plaited in the basic plait just described by tying the five plaiting straws at the head of the core, and continuing the plaiting right up to the other end and on until a short length of braid is ready to curve round and down to make a loop for hanging it up. Weave the straw ends neatly into the body of the dolly to finish off.

A different appearance can be achieved by using more straws in the plait, bringing the corner folds closer together. Remember that however many straws you decide to use you will have one corner less (seven straws make six corner folds, eight straws make seven, etc.). You can trim the dolly with braid loops. Another variation is the Welsh Border Dolly which is a traditional Neck trimmed with two lengths of five straw plait made without a core.

The traditional Neck figures in all harvest ceremonies both in the field and at the supper. Devonshire had a special ceremony in which the dolly had to be smuggled into the farmhouse without the maids catching the man who had it. If they did both man and dolly were showered with water.

A very special traditional Neck dolly is worked in double plait which produces an unusual effect. Instead of the straws running straight from corner fold to corner fold, in this complicated plait the straws go behind every other corner fold to give the appearance as shown in Fig. 4 of the enlarged section of the dolly. One must do two rounds of plaiting to make one pattern, each round using only half the straws. This plait can only be worked with an even number of straws and looks best if plaited without a core. The dolly illustrated was made by Mr Dabinett of Curry Rivel, Somerset, who thinks he has worked out a new plait and so we have named it the Dabinett Somerset Neck. Here are directions for working with eight straws, although it can be done with ten, twelve or more. It is important to remember that each straw is folded over the next three instead of the usual two corner folds. Pick up the first straw and take over straws Nos 2, 3, and 4. Then pick up the fourth, fold it over Nos 1, 5, and 6, No 6 then passes over Nos 4, 7 and 8. Next take No 8 over Nos 6, 2 and 3. This is the first round and half the straws have been used. Straw No 3 passes over Nos 8,

Fig. 4. Dabinett
Somerset Neck.

1 and 5 and No 5 on being picked up folds over Nos 3, 4 and 7. To complete one pattern pick up No 7 and fold it over Nos 5, 6, and 2. Then straw No 2 folds over straws Nos 7, 8 and 1. Repeat the whole sequence. The finishing braid loop for this dolly is exactly the same as for the traditional one already given.

There are many ways of giving an individual look to small dollies such as are seen in modern sitting rooms. Using a different number of straws will change the look of the finished object but the spiral will always be there. One way to get softer curves is to use a pencil or length of round wooden rod for the core. By plaiting round such an object then removing it, you are left with a tube of plaited work which is a simple thing to bend into almost any shape. If you want a perfect ring put your loop to dry held in shape on a suitable pot or jar. If you require a firm shape do your plaiting round long lengths of straw (which remain in the dolly). 7 or 8 straws will give a core of the right size for a twelve-inch length of work which makes a single loop or a small three-sided dolly. After plaiting up the straws place it on a table and divide with a ruler to make three sides; bend this carefully with the fingers, bringing the two ends together and tie; finish off with a bow of ribbon. There are many variations of this shape. Plaiting can be done with four straws which gives three corner folds or with any other number, but always start at the top under the ears (see plate 2).

All corn dollies should have some ears of corn incorporated in the design. This recalls the old belief that the corn spirit, having slept in the seeds during the winter, awoke in the spring and passed into the newly sown seed in the fields.

# 3. Countryman's favours

Years ago young country lads took their special girl for a walk through the fields after the evening service in church. At harvest time just before the reaping began, the young man would plait a short length of braid and twist it into a knot as a buttonhole for his sweetheart. These braids can be made with two, three or four straws as illustrated in figures 5 to 8. These braids are still popular in Scotland where the plaiters use the finest rye stems to make intricate knots into brooches.

### Two straw plait

A useful braid can be made with two straws. Tie them together just below the ears and, with the ears hanging downwards between the fingers of the left hand, fold the two long straws out until they

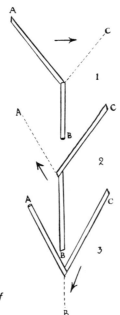

*Fig. 5. Diagrams of two straw plait.*

form a right angle to the ears — one straw out to point A and the other to point B as in Fig. 5 (1). Take the straw at A, being careful not to bend or crack it except at the centre tie, and fold it over until it rests at point C. Follow this by folding the straw at B in the same way until it rests at the point left empty by straw A. The third move is to take the straw from point C and fold it over into the gap left by B. This forms one round and the straws are ready at points A and B for repeating.

**'Cat's Paw' three straw plait**

Tie together three straws at the base of the ears and spread out to positions of Fig.6 (1). Pick up first straw A and carry over in a half circle until it lies at the outside of B as in Fig.6 (2). B is next taken over in a similar movement until it lies in the position A left, Fig.6 (3). Now take straw C and fold over until it lies at the side of A but without folding over it, Fig. 6 (4). Then pick up A and, folding it over C, bring it into the position left by C.

This braid is useful for buttonholes and also for trimming large dollies. When correctly plaited it is tighter than the hair braid and has a decided ridge up the centre.

**Another three straw plait**

This is a very simple plait similar to the four straw one. Work with three straws as shown in Fig. 7, remembering always that each straw must return to its original place if the plait is to retain the symmetry which forms the attractive pattern.

**Four straw plait**

Tie four straws together below the ears and, holding the work in

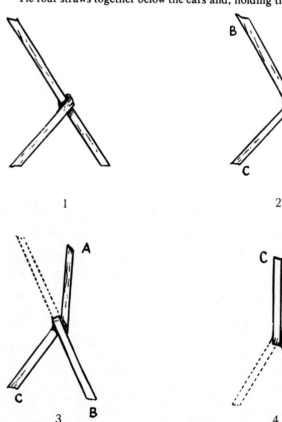

the left hand, fold the straws out until at right angles to the ears, which hang down between the fingers. As can be seen in Fig. 8 straws A and C must fold over and change places, the straws B and D do the same in each round. The correct way to do this is by bringing each straw in turn up and over in a half circle until it lies once more at right angles to the ears. It is important to make sure each straw returns to its original place in the following rounds, as shown in the diagram.

**The Glory**

In one of my earlier books I introduced the idea of making a slightly larger design from these braids, which comes in very

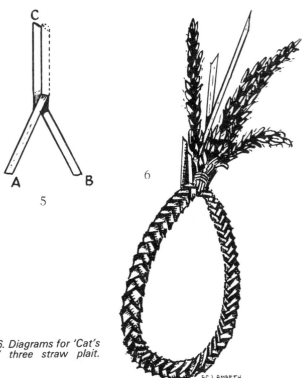

Fig. 6. Diagrams for 'Cat's Paw' three straw plait.

R.C. LAMBETH.

# THREE STRAW PLAIT

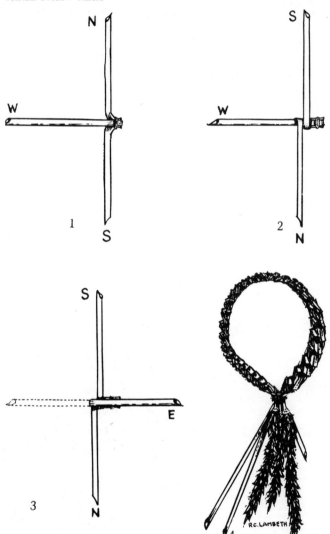

*Fig. 7. Diagrams for second variety of three straw plait.*

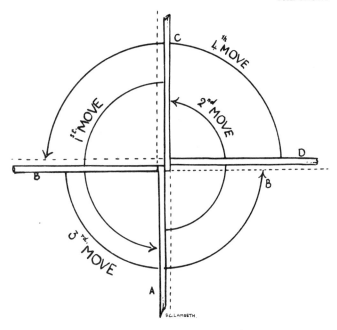

*Fig. 8. Diagram for four straw plait.*

useful for decorating the church at harvest time. This I gave the name of Glory because it reminds one of the light shown behind the heads of saints in church windows. It is easily made in a very short time with three strand hair plait but it can be made more elaborate by using the various wide, flat hat braids. (Some of these will be found in the bigger instruction book *A Golden Dolly*.) For the simple braid tie fifteen straws (which still have their ears) together just below them. The plait is worked with the ears towards you and the straws away out in front. Divide them into three groups and carefully fold each group in turn until about six inches of braid have been made, then tie them all together and fold the ends up behind the work, fanning them out to support the corn ears. If the straw ends are too short to make a good fan use a group of plaiting straws for the purpose but tie them in the same way as butterfly wings, only keep the tie at one end instead of at the middle of the straws.

19

Fig. 9. 'Glory'.

# 4. Traditional designs

### The Mare

The Mare is rather quaint but it does give us some idea of how the people of the middle ages made many of their corn emblems. It is, as far as I know, entirely English and Fig. 10 gives a good idea of the way they tied that last handful up to represent a Mare. This type of dolly was made in Shropshire, Hertfordshire and Herefordshire we know but it is quite possible that it was made in all counties where corn was grown. In the Isle of Skye this figure was made but it was known as the Cripple Goat although the custom of its use is the same.

Before the enclosure of land, when the only division between one farmer's land and that of his neighbour was a ridge or dyke, the first farmer to get all his corn harvested made a Mare and sent it to a neighbour who had corn still standing. The young man who took it had to be spry for he would be chased by the reapers because no one wanted the straw figure as it suggested they were slow workers. Each farmer who received it made haste to finish his harvest and pass the Mare to someone else. This passing-on only stopped when all harvest was gathered in, and the man who had the Mare had to keep it. It was thought that horses would know who had the Mare and feed from his stacks, leaving other farmers' stores of grain untouched.

A custom in Hertfordshire and Shropshire was to Cry the Mare. For this, the straw figure was stood in the centre of the field and all the reapers threw their sickles at it. When someone succeeded in cutting the knot of the straw rope binding it a cry of 'Mare' went up and the successful man received the sheaf as a prize. Around Hitchin farmers did not always pass on the last handful cut but raced home with it hoping to reach safety before any villager could throw water over it to 'drown' the evil spirit hiding in it.

## The Staffordshire Knot

Another amusing story is told by the people of Staffordshire about their knot and, of course, this well-known knot is used as their corn dolly. (It appears on lamp posts, as a regimental badge

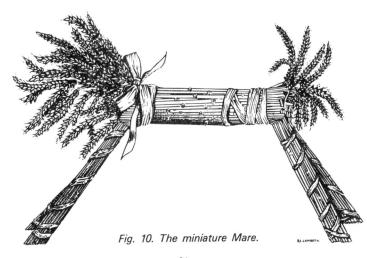

*Fig. 10. The miniature Mare.*

on the caps of the county regiment and with the Coat of Arms.) Once there were three vagabonds due to be hanged but there was only one gallows, so the three were told that if they could devise a knot which would hang them all at one go, they would be reprieved!

To make a good sized knot use a piece of round wooden rod of a half-inch diameter. Only a short length is required for it can be pulled up as the plait grows. Start by tying five (or six) straws just below the ears and spread them out as for the basic plait. Then work a few widening out rounds until there is room to insert the end of the rod. Work up this until the braid is 28 inches long; then do a few rounds to bring the braid in narrower and insert the same number of ears in this as you have at the beginning. Tie them and the plaiting straw together. Once this has been done, carefully

*Fig. 11. The Staffordshire Knot.*

*Fig. 12. Northamptonshire Horns.*

curve the hollow braid round as in Fig. 11 and fasten the ends in place. Add a good bunch of corn and a bow of ribbon.

## Horns

It is natural when giving a gift to make it as beautiful as possible; hence the decorating of first the sacrifice, then in more civilised times the corn and fruit of harvest. One of the earliest designs used was the horn, or cornucopia, partly because horns were a symbol of the gods but also because horns were in general use in the home for drinking vessels and for calling up cattle.

Northamptonshire people use a pair of horns decorated with ears of wheat and barley for their corn dolly (Fig. 12). There are many ways of plaiting a single harvest horn. Some plaiters work on a wire frame which gives support for the bouquet of seeds and fruit; others plait round a paper cone and curve their dolly into shape afterwards; others plait double by starting the horn at the tip and then, when long enough, plaiting back over their own work (but it produces a rather clumsy design).

Most counties had a favourite design which they claimed as their own, although some designs were common to several. Yorkshire, Durham, Lancashire and Lincolnshire all made a chandelier, whilst Norfolk and Herefordshire made a lan-

23

*Fig. 13. The Cambridgeshire Handbell.*

tern. Rumania, Greece and some countries in South America also make lanterns although in each case there are slight differences in design.

### The Cambridgeshire handbell

Cambridgeshire adopted the handbell as its dolly. When bringing home the last load of the harvest from the fields the journey became a procession of rejoicing, with the men ringing handbells, everyone singing songs, and children riding on the load on which the last handful of corn, in the form of a dolly, had the place of honour. This was kept until the following harvest when it was either fed to the cattle to help the animals produce good calves or burnt to ensure that no old seed was saved.

The Cambridgeshire handbell, Fig. 13, is made on a ten-inch core with seven wheat ears for the clapper. Plaiting starts at the ears with five straws. Work about four inches up the core then tie off the last straw folded and fold the other four back down the plaited part until required (Fig. 14). Next take five more plaiting straws and tie at the tip of the handle with the ends turned in. Work until the two lengths of plait meet. Now, using the first four and the second five straws work with all nine to plait the bell cup,

1. A basket showing the use of spider web plaiting.

2. This bow corn dolly is made on a core of seven long straws with wheat ears, plaiting is with five straws and the bow is bent into shape after plaiting. The extra corn is added just before the ribbon is tied in place.

3. A straw Bell from Guatemala, made by Manuel Palux, aged eleven.

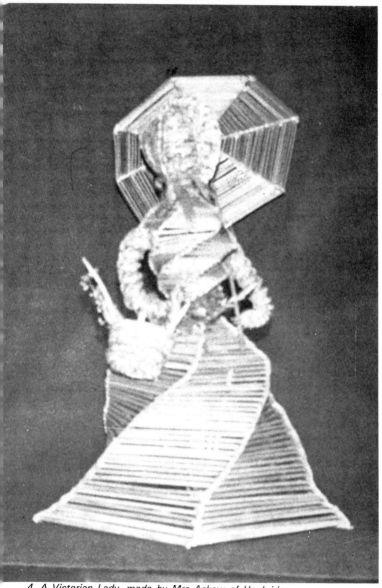

4. A Victorian Lady, made by Mrs Askew of Heybridge, Maldon, Essex.

5. A Greek Lantern.

6. An Indian Ram's Horn made with rice straw.

7. A modern way of using straw.

8. A trinket Tray made with two straw braid and a flat hat braid, in the Museum of English Rural Life.

9. Stars and small plaited ornaments made with Artstraws and drinking straws.

shaping it with the widening technique. There is no core to help with this cup; you must rely on your own eyes and hands. Do not attempt it, therefore, until you are reasonably proficient.

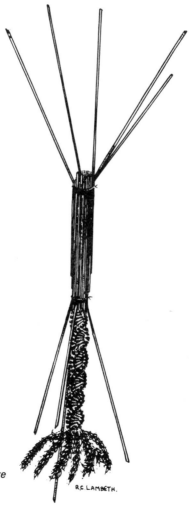

*Fig. 14. Bell core and plait.*

R.C. LAMBETH.

*Fig. 15. Cambridgeshire Umbrella.*

R.C. LAMBETH.

34

## The Cambridgeshire umbrella

Another Cambridgeshire dolly is the umbrella (Fig. 15), and for this a length of strong wire must be used to form the handle. This is covered with a few padding straws, then more short straws added for the main part of the umbrella. The five straw plait is used for the handle starting at the tip and two (or three) extra plaiting straws added when starting on the body. At this point one can insert six or eight wheat ears round the handle base to represent knobs on the ends of the ribs.

## The crook

Although we do not think of sheep as part of the harvest they do give a 'harvest' of wool at sheep shearing which takes place a little earlier. It is not surprising, therefore, to find a corn dolly in the shape of the shepherd's crook, also used by bishops on some ceremonial occasions. The one drawn in Fig. 16 is of simple design being made on a five foot length of thick, stiff wire padded with five or six straws. The crook top is decorated with wheat and a symbolic crown round the neck finishes off the work. Many people make these in basic five straw plait starting at one end and working until the whole staff is covered but I prefer to work first from the top curve to the neck with five straw plait, and then to plait from the bottom with seven straws until the two lots of plait meet. This leaves a number of straws ready for plaiting the crown. This is worked by using the widening technique until it is the desired size; the straw ends are then used to make lengths of two straw braid for the loops round the crown's rim.

## The Suffolk horseshoe

Although we always think of Suffolk as the home of the horse-shoe corn dolly, because of its association with the Suffolk Punch working horse, the shoe is made in many other areas. The horseshoe lends itself to a variety of designs: it can be made to any size and can be trimmed with one or two carters' whips (not riding switches) or a bunch of corn (Fig. 17). Horseshoes must have a wire in the core, because without it the shape loses the inward curving ends. A medium-sized shoe can be made with a wire sixteen inches long, padded with about fourteen lengths of straw and covered with five or six straw plait. First tie the plaiting straws very tightly to the core, making sure the ends are turned inwards. On reaching the other end fold the plaiting straws over to cover the end of the core, then slot them through the corner folds. A strong, large-eyed wool needle is very useful for this work.

*Fig. 16. Shepherd's Crook.*

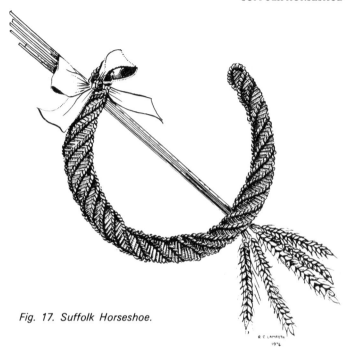

*Fig. 17. Suffolk Horseshoe.*

**The crown**

A crown makes a very good corn dolly for the church Harvest Festival but this, again, requires a wire frame and it is possible to get these made by wireworkers. The one in Fig. 18 is twelve inches wide and eight inches high (not including the braid ornament at the top). The narrow curves are covered with the five straw plait but the base is padded and eight straws were used in the plait. The braids of the wheat ears which decorate this are the Cat's Paw plait, and two straw plait is used for the top ornament and at the centre base. A backing of red or purple card helps to show off this silhouette. It is also possible to make a 'round' crown. This only requires one wire ring for the base, for the upper part can be made with five or seven straws using the basic plait

37

and a bunch of corn for the centre. Ribbon and a velvet cap help to make this crown a de-luxe model.

The crown does not belong to England only; it was also made in Poland as the climax of the harvest ingathering. The Polish crown was a very elaborate thing which included something from all sections of country life and was worn by the leading girl of the harvest procession. The Polish harvest usually began on St Lawrence's Day, early in August, and the crown, which was made soon afterwards, was taken to the church to be blessed before the leading girl was crowned. She later received a gift from the head man in exchange for the crown.

### The Pickering chalice

Yorkshire, like one or two other counties, makes some very fine corn dollies as well as the harvest Dame. The Pickering chalice is one of the most interesting designs because of its association with early Christianity. It is based on the Communion cup and was originally made very tall. A version suitable for today's homes should be about eighteen inches from the base to the top of the bouquet of corn. The vessel should have some weight in the bottom, otherwise it becomes top heavy. I have used metal discs for this but a very small jar is better, for this can be used both as a weight and a holder for the stems of the corn. The best number of straws for plaiting this design is nine because this gives a good round shape and makes eight corner folds. As there are four small 'tablets' to be hung from the rim, this divides evenly. I am told that the tablets represent those brought down the mountain by Moses. These are made with the spider web plait using two crossed straws and plaiting with one straw at a time.

### The Yorkshire candlestick

Another Yorkshire dolly is based on the brass candlestick of the eighteenth and nineteenth centuries. It makes a good dolly for standing as against those which hang up. The candle is made separately on a few straws, one of which must have the ear left on to represent the flame. Plaiting starts at the top of the candle which should not be too thick for it must fit into the cup of the candlestick. The holder requires about five plain straws for the core and work starts at the bottom with seven straws being tied tightly with the ends up the core. Plait with the widening technique, keeping the work flat on the table and working out as quickly as possible. (Do not let the work 'dish' up.) The base should be about three and a half inches in diameter, and when it is large enough start to work up the holder by keeping two or three rounds of plait straight up, then using the narrowing technique to

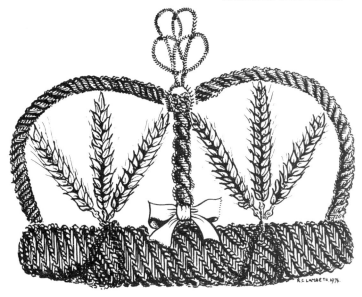

*Fig. 18. The Crown.*

make the work close in until it reaches the core. After this you can make any number of curves to please yourself until the height you want is reached, but remember to allow for the cup at the top. This has no core so that the candle will fit into it after the rim is plaited. To finish off the straws take the bottom one at the corner where there are two but bring it up in front of the top straw and fold to the left; tie this off to the previous corner fold. Next take the other straw from the same corner fold over in the usual direction and tie at the next corner and leave. Repeat this corner until you reach the first tie you made and here you tie the three after crossing them. Cut off all ends and fit the candle into the holder.

### The Essex terret

Essex has a special corn dolly known as the terret. This curved, double-ended dolly is based on part of the trimmings of horses' harness. Years ago the crown piece of the harness carried a half hoop of brass between the animal's ears and this was decorated with small bells or tassels. The core for this dolly has a good bunch of corn at both ends and it should be padded with extra straw on one side only which will be the top of the curve when finished. The terret is plaited with six straws because there is some strain when the dolly is pulled into a curve and tied with cotton until the straw dries, when the cotton can be removed.

## Mother Earth

All harvest traditions have something of the female in them, either as a goddess or simply as 'Mother Earth' who is responsible for the growing plants.

There are many designs of harvest dolls. There is the Kern Babby of Whalton in Northumberland, made each year by a member of the same family for the church Harvest Festival. There is the Ivy Girl of Kent, representative of Ceres to the Romans and Demeter to the Greeks. In Peru a female figure, Pirva, was made of maize and richly adorned for their ceremony, while Scandinavian countries make straw figures of the Virgin Mary for their Christmas decorations. Angels are made in almost every country where there is straw. Mexico produces a whole orchestra, for their angels have different instruments, and Czechoslovakia makes marvellous small figures from the outer covering of sweet corn.

Mother Earth is not difficult to make (Fig. 19). The arms are made first on a small core with a few ears of corn at both ends for the hands. Then eight or ten very straight straws form the centre of the body twelve inches long. Plaiting starts at the top of the head using seven straws. Fit the arms up the middle of the core when the shoulders are reached then carry on widening or drawing in the rounds of plaiting as required. To finish off the skirt fold all straw to the core and tie.

This figure can be provided with a base of wood in a very simple way. Before plaiting begins on the head and body take a length of firm wire about an inch longer than the centre core, make a very small loop at the top then put the wire down the centre of the core. Three quarters of an inch of wire will show at the bottom of the core and when the figure has been plaited drill a hole the same size as the wire in a small block of wood and press the wire down into this until it fits very tightly.

## Herefordshire and Welsh fans

Choose twenty-five wheat or rye straws with good ears, either all the ears being the same size, or if of different sizes graded with the three largest for the centre point, the beginning of the plaiting, and the smallest at the end. Before work begins remember to soak the straws well, preferably in cold water. Tie the first three ears together letting them remain flat on the table and parallel to each other while tying. Do not bunch them up.

Fig. 19. Mother Earth.

Use a sheet of newspaper to work on and if there is a line on it make that the centre of your fan. Visually it will look like this: three ears at the base of the line close to you, with the long straws opening out on each side of the line to form a V, two to the left and one to the right. With the work always flat on the table, lift the outside left hand straw until it is at right angles to the table but the ear remains flat, pass this straw over the second straw and bring down on the inside of the straw on the right. This gives two straws at the right hand side. Pick up the outer one and as before bring down inside the one on the left.

*Repeat from here.* Add two more straws by lifting first the outside left hand straw just enough to slip one straw under it with the length of new straw running over all straws on the left and up the V to the inside on the right. Make sure it is close to the other right hand straw. Then, working from the right, put the second straw in place in the same way. Next, work two folds up each side — first, one at the left by picking up the second straw from the outside and holding it upright while you take the outside straw round at table level until it lies on the inside of the right hand straws. Replace the upright straw in the place it came from and it will hold firmly in place the straw you have just moved. Repeat the process working from the right, then again first from the left, then the right, keeping an eye on the V to see that both sides are equal. Continue with the plaiting by returning each time to *repeat from here* until all the ears have been used. After this make six or seven more folds up each side without adding extra straws. Tie each group of straws three inches from the centre. Two lengths of two straw plait can be made from the ends of these straws (one each) or a long length from two new straws to make a loop for hanging up the fan.

A variation of this fan can be made to look like a quill by the following method. Start your fan in the usual way and work until there are nine ears in place, finishing with the two folds at each side. Instead of putting the next pair of ears (10 and 11) under the outside straws put them under the second straw in; this leaves the outside straws unused. Repeat the usual folds at each side, inserting the ears under the second straw, not the first. Each time an extra pair of ears is inserted the two outside straws are left unused. These are cut off when all the plaiting is finished. To finish the top you can either fold all straws together after the usual number of folds after all ears have been used, or you can continue the folds leaving the outside straw as before after two folds each side until left with just enough straws to plait into a loop.

### Religious emblems

Because one of the important duties of all corn dollies is to offer thanks to God for our harvests, there are a number of traditional designs such as the Cross of Our Lord, the crosses of St George and St Andrew, the beautiful Devonshire Cross and Crown, the Keys of St Peter and the Anchor of St Clement which will always be in demand for the Harvest Festival. There is also a quaint belief among some plaiters that their corn dollies should only have seven corn ears in them in memory of the 'seven years of plenty' from the Old Testament.

### 'Lost' designs

For a period of time plaiting declined because of the dying of the straw hat trade and changes in the characteristics of straw resulting from the use of the combine, and we have therefore lost some of the county designs. One or two of these remain with us as names only. What shape was the 'Little Moppett' of Somerset or the Jack and Jill of Bedfordshire? The latter was most probably a double-headed traditional dolly.

### Double-ended dollies

Double-ended corn dollies can be found in a number of other counties and do make a variant to the traditional Neck,

*Fig. 20. Herefordshire Fan.*

R.C.LAMBETH. 1974.

especially if the plaiting is done with the reversing twist. Make up a core with a good bunch of corn ears at both ends and add one or two rounds of extra straw to the middle length of the core. Next measure the core for length, decide how many times you want to reverse the direction of the spiral, divide the number of inches and mark the core so that each change over will produce a piece of plaiting of the same size. Start the plait at one end with six straws and work to the point of change. You can either turn the work upside-down and continue the rounds by working under, instead of over, two corner folds each time, or you can keep your work the right way up and change from plaiting to the right in an anti-clockwise direction to plaiting to the left in a clockwise direction. This gives a very good dolly.

## Modern designs

Although modern in design these dollies are made with traditional plaits. Because plaiters must keep up with present day trends, many new designs are appearing in craft shops and at church harvest festivals. One of the first people to realise the modern use of straw plaits was the late Mr Mizen of Great Bardfield in Essex, when he made the Royal Arms in straw for the Festival of Britain in 1951. His work created great interest and a new era began for straw work.

Since that time many new shapes and designs have appeared: models of guns made by Neville Bonner, the seahorse by Barry Bonner, the snail and its shell by the Reverend Basil Turner, Norwich Cathedral modelled entirely in straw by Elizabeth Smith, who also makes the rickshaw, the Ely octagon star where I introduced the use of geometric design with plain straw, the eel glave, and the marquetry shield of the three crowns of East Anglia, now illustrated in *Straw Craft: More Golden Dollies*. All this indicates that straw craft is becoming one of the new arts while at the same time being a revival of a traditional craft.

## Straw marquetry

For those with patience there is another aspect of straw work, the marquetry straw pictures and decorated boxes introduced into this country by French prisoners during the Napoleonic Wars. The best straw for this work is the thicker, second length of straw after the top length has been cut off for plaiting. This straw requires rather longer soaking and when this has been done each straw must be split down one side and ironed on the inner side with a hot iron to flatten it out. Draw a simple picture on cardboard and cut pieces of straw into the shapes to fit the objects in your picture. Modern transparent glues work very well with straw.

*Fig. 21. Stack cockerel.*

### Stack ornaments

Stack ornaments are not plaited but are made by folding the straw and tying it with binder twine or strong grass. It is possible to make a good cockerel in this way by carefully folding the straw and using twine to hold the tail erect as in Fig. 21. Other stack figures include crowns, weather vanes, crosses, pheasants and foxes. Some thatchers use chicken wire to cover their work to stop birds removing straw. Originally these ornaments were put up 'to stop the witches landing on the stacks'.

### Scandinavian Christmas straw work

In the group of countries which form Scandinavia much of their straw work is not plaited but tied with bright red or natural cotton. Items like the Star of David, small figures and lozenge shapes are made for Christmas scenes while the sunflower plays an important part in their mid-summer festivals. Very effective figures are made of simple three strand straw hair braid tied and bent into shape while damp. Finland makes a very good goat of straw in much the same way that stack ornaments are made.

I have seen straw animals which came from Germany but these were tied into bundles and then clipped into shape.

# 5. Designs for Artstraws and drinking straws

Many of the designs in the book could be made with the new 'Artstraws' for these unwaxed paper straws make a good substitute for straw, especially if one lives in a busy town where it is difficult to find the hollow straw needed for traditional plaiting. Artstraws are much longer than drinking straws and one can use spray paints to colour them. They are ideal for teachers who need to show their pupils where each straw goes as one plaits and they are just that much thicker than the real thing, which helps give confidence to the beginner. They will not take the place of good hollow plaiting straw entirely for there is a quality about real straw which fascinates the plaiter once he, or she, has used it.

All the smaller designs used for mobiles and the Christmas stars look well made with Artstraws (see plate 9) but Angels and figures for Christmas scenes do come up somewhat larger than in straw so it is as well to work out their size and then make the background to fit.

### German stars

These instructions for making stars apply to both paper or real straw. A piece of wood approximately five inches square and thirty-two headless nails are all that is required. Mark a ring four inches in diameter on the wood and knock in the nails spacing them at intervals of about three eighths of an inch. Take eight straws and place them in the templet, the first two making a cross and each additional straw dividing the gaps thus left. When all eight straws are in correct position you will see that every other space between the nails has been used. Draw a thread under every other straw and over the ones in between. Then pull it tight and fasten off securely. Make a second star with eight more straws, and return both stars to the frame making sure the top one fills the gaps in the ring of nails left by the first star. Put a strong thread round as before, using the ends to make a loop for hanging up. Trim the ends of the straw to a point.

### Butterflies, dragonflies and tassels

These can be made with both kinds of straw. First make a pair of wings by placing seven or eight lengths of straw side by side on the table with a thread wrapped twice round the centre. Place two fingers of one hand flat over them with both ends of the thread coming up between them. Take the ends in the other hand and pull gently but firmly until very tight. At the same time you will see the ends of the straws spread out into fans. Do not allow the straws to 'jump up' into a bunch while drawing the thread tight, they must remain flat, side by side all the time. For the tassels just trim one half of the wings shorter than the other and both halves to a point at the centre. For the butterfly and dragonfly take two long straws and fold in half, slip a very short piece of straw into the fold for the antennae and tie in place. Place the pair of wings up the body, half the body straws above and half below, and tie firmly in place. Trim the edges of the wings into shape and cut the end of the body to a point. These two can be given a gay look by the use of coloured embroidery thread woven round the wing straws.

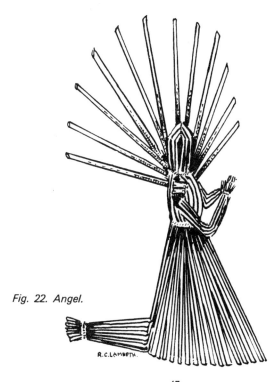

Fig. 22. Angel.

R.C.LAMBETH.

**Angels**

Angel wings are made in the same way but with longer straws and a very straight wire slotted in the first straw. When the thread is pulled tight the straws will fan out away from the one containing the wire. Having tied the thread off, make a mock machine stitched half circle about half an inch across to keep all the straws in place then bend the straws into a V with the one wired straw on the outer edge. Tie together three or four straws of suitable length for a pair of arms. Next take a bunch of straws for the head and body; these are tied together at the centre then carefully folded down until the tie is at the top of the head. Now tie a thread round the whole group for the neck and slip the arms up into place. Take two extra straws and fold over the arms for each shoulder, fit the wings up under three or four of the body straws at the back and tie strongly round the waist. Trim all straws to make the angel stand and shape the wing edges. A kneeling figure can be made in the same way but the straws for the back of the body must be left longer than the front and two lengths of wire must be inserted up it to keep the 'legs' in a kneeling position.

# 6. Further reading

Johnson, Doris, and Coker, Alec. *Complete Book of Strawcraft and Corn Dollies*. Dover, 1987.

Lambeth, M. *A Golden Dolly*. John Baker, 1969.

Lambeth, M. *A New Golden Dolly*. 1966.

Lambeth, M. *The Golden Dolly*. 1963.

Lambeth, M. *Straw Craft: More Golden Dollies*. John Baker, 1974.

Parsons, Trish, and Dufour, Peter. *Corn Dollies*. Search Press, 1983.

Sandford, Lettice, and Davis, Philla. *Decorative Straw Work*. 1964.

Staniforth, Arthur. *Straw and Straw Craftsmen*. Shire, 1991.